MFK FISHER

Consider the Oyster

NORTH POINT PRESS
Farrar, Straus and Giroux
New York

North Point Press
A division of Farrar, Straus and Giroux
19 Union Square West, New York 10003

Distributed in Canada by Douglas & McIntyre Ltd.
Printed in the United States of America
First North Point Press edition, 1988

Library of Congress Control Number: 88-61169
ISBN-13: 978-0-86547-335-5
ISBN-10: 0-86547-335-8

Designed by David Bullen

www.fsgbooks.com

18   17   16   15   14

For Dillwyn Parrish

Contents

He was a bold man that first eat an oyster.

Polite Conversation, JONATHAN SWIFT

Consider
the Oyster

Love and Death
Among the Molluscs

. . . Secret, and self-contained, and solitary as an oyster.
A Christmas Carol, CHARLES DICKENS

An oyster leads a dreadful but exciting life.

Indeed, his chance to live at all is slim, and if he should survive the arrows of his own outrageous fortune and in the two weeks of his carefree youth find a clean smooth place to fix on, the years afterwards are full of stress, passion, and danger.

He—but why make him a he, except for clarity? Almost any normal oyster never knows from one year to the next whether he is he or she, and may start at any moment, after the first year, to lay eggs where before he spent his sexual energies in being exceptionally masculine. If he is a she, her energies are equally feminine, so that in a single summer, if all goes well, and the temperature of the water is somewhere around or above seventy degrees, she may spawn several hundred million eggs, fifteen to one hundred million at a time, with commendable pride.

American oysters differ as much as American people, so that

the Atlantic Coast inhabitants spend their childhood and adolescence floating free and unprotected with the tides, conceived far from their mothers and their fathers too by milt let loose in the water near the eggs, while the Western oysters lie within special brood-chambers of the maternal shell, inseminated and secure, until they are some two weeks old. The Easterners seem more daring.

A little oyster is born, then, in the water. At first, about five to ten hours after he and at least a few hundred thousand of his mother's eggs have been fertilized by his potent and unknown sire, he is merely a larva. He is small, but he is free-swimming . . . and he swims thus freely for about two weeks, wherever the tides and his peculiar whims may lead him. He is called a spat.

It is to be hoped, sentimentally at least, that the spat—*our* spat—enjoys himself. Those two weeks are his one taste of vagabondage, of devil-may-care free roaming. And even they are not quite free, for during all his youth he is busy growing a strong foot and a large supply of sticky cementlike stuff. If he thought, he might wonder why.

The two weeks up, he suddenly attaches himself to the first clean hard object he bumps into. His fifty million brothers who have not been eaten by fish may or may not bump into anything clean and hard, and those who do not, die. But our spat has been lucky, and in great good spirits he clamps himself firmly to his home, probably forever. He is by now about one-seventy-fifth of an inch long, whatever that may be . . . and he is an oyster.

Since he is an Easterner, a Chincoteague or a Lynnhaven maybe, he has found a pleasant, moderately salty bottom, where the tides wash regularly and there is no filth to pollute him and no sand to choke him.

There he rests, tied firmly by his left foot, which seems to have become a valve in the immutable way of all oyster feet. He devotes himself to drinking, and rapidly develops an enviable capacity, so that in good weather, when the temperature stays near seventy-eight degrees, he can easily handle twenty-six or - seven quarts an hour. He manages better than most creatures to combine business with pleasure, and from this stream of water that passes through his gills he strains out all the delicious little diatoms and peridia that are his food.

His home—we are speaking now of domesticated oysters— is a wire bag full of old shells, or perhaps a cement-coated pole planted by a wily oyster-farmer. Or perhaps it is what the government describes winningly as "a particularly efficient collector," which is made from an egg-crate partition coated with a mixture of lime and cement.

Whatever the anchorage (and I hope, sentimentally again, that it is at least another shell, since because he is an Easterner our little spat can never know the esthetic pleasure of finding a bamboo stick in Japan, nor a hollow tile laid out especially for him in France or Portugal), whatever the anchorage, spat-dom is over and done with. The two fine free-swimming weeks are forever gone, maturity with all its cares has come, and an oyster, according to Richard Sheridan's *Critic*, may be crossed in love.

For about a year this oyster—*our* oyster—is a male, fertilizing a few hundred thousand eggs as best he can without ever knowing whether they swim by or not. Then one day, maternal longings surge between his two valves in his cold guts and gills and all his crinkly fringes. Necessity, that well-known mother, makes him one. He is a she.

From then on she, with occasional vacations of being masculine just to keep her hand in, bears her millions yearly. She is in the full bloom of womanhood when she is about seven.

She is a fine plump figure of an oyster, plumper still in the summer when the season and her instincts get the better of her. She has traveled some, thanks to cupidinous farmers who have subjected her to this tide and that, this bed and that, for their own mean ends. She has grown into a gray-white oval shape, with shades of green or ocher or black in her gills and a rudimentary brain in the forepart of her blind deaf body. She can feel shadows as well as the urgency of milt, and her delicate muscles know danger and pull shut her shells with firmness.

Danger is everywhere for her, and extermination lurks. (How do we know with what pains? How can we tell or not tell the sufferings of an oyster? There is a brain . . .) She is the prey of many enemies, and must lie immobile as a fungus while the starfish sucks her and the worm bores.

She has eight enemies, not counting man who is the greatest, since he protects her from the others only to eat her himself.

The first enemy is the starfish, which floats hungrily in all the Eastern tides and at last wraps arms about the oyster like a hideous lover and forces its shells apart steadily and then thrusts his stomach into it and digests it. The picture is ugly. The oyster is left bare as any empty shell, and the starfish floats on, hungry still. (Men try to catch it with things called star-mops.)

The second enemy, almost as dangerous, is a kind of snail called a screw-borer, or an oyster drill. It bores wee round holes in the shells, and apparently worries the poor mollusc enough to make men invent traps for it: wire bags baited with seed-oysters catch it, but none too efficiently, since it remains a menace.

Then there is a boring sponge. It makes tiny tunnels all through the shell like honeycomb, until an oyster becomes thin and weak from trying to stop up all the holes, and then is often smothered by the sponge from the outside, so that you know what Louisa May Alcott meant when she wrote, "Now I am beginning to live a little, and feel less like a sick oyster at low tide."

There are wafers, or leeches, and "Black Drums." And mussels too will smother oysters or starve them by coming to stay on their shells and eating all their food. Out on the Pacific Coast, slipper shells, which are somewhat fancily called *Crepidula fornicata*, will go the mussels one better. And even ducks, flying here and there as ducks must, land long enough to make themselves a disastrously good meal occasionally on an oyster bed.

Life is hard, we say. An oyster's life is worse. She lives motionless, soundless, her own cold ugly shape her only dissipation, and if she escapes the menace of duck-slipper-mussel-Black-Drum-leech-sponge-borer-starfish, it is for man to eat, because of man's own hunger.

Men have enjoyed eating oysters since they were not much more than monkeys, according to the kitchen middens they have left behind them. And thus, in their own one-minded way, they have spent time and thought and money on the problems of how to protect oysters from the suckers and the borers and the starvers, until now it is comparatively easy to eat this two-valved mollusc anywhere, without thought of the dangers it has run in its few years. Its chilly, delicate gray body slips into a stewpan or under a broiler or alive down a red throat, and it is done. Its life has been thoughtless but no less full of danger, and now that it is over we are perhaps the better for it.

A Supper to Sleep On

Oysters are very unsatisfactory food for labouring men, but will do for the sedentary, and for a supper to sleep on.

The Philosophy of Eating, A. J. BELLOWS, 1870

There are several different kinds of stews. A stew can be a sweat or a welter in hot close atmosphere or, according to the English dictionaries, a swot. It can be a tank or pond for storing live fish. It can be a brothel.

It can be something cooked by long simmering in a closed vessel with little liquid in it. And there are probably several other things a stew can be, but even the American lexicographers seem ignorant of one of the best; have they never heard of an oyster stew?

Is it possible that they never knew, when they were children, the cozy pleasure of Sunday night supper in wintertime, when crackers and the biggest tureen of steaming buttery creamy oyster stew stood on the table, and were plenty?

Is it possible that when they grew somewhat older, those be-nighted men never went to Doylestown in Pennsylvania to get married or something, and thus never sat voluptuously at the

Inn's dim oyster bar while their stew was flicked together before them in two or three little copper pans?

Is it possible that, sometime after the first joys of maturity and before they grew old enough to write dictionaries, those men never sat with a few friends and compared, solemnly and delightfully, their various methods of making oyster stews themselves?

It is possible, poor souls, and it is even probable, for how else could they print their sweeping statements about "long simmering in a closed vessel with little liquid" and not at least add "*except* oyster stew"?

Even a child knows as much if he has ever watched, a few times in his early winters, the simple making of his Sunday supper. He remembers the recipe too, partly because it is so simple and partly because no matter how long he lives afterwards, its recollection will add to what well-being he has or perhaps may once have had.

In spite of its simplicity, oyster stew has several formulae, or rather methods of putting together, since the ingredients are almost constant. Rich milk, butter, salt, pepper, and of course, oysters, make up every recipe I ever heard . . . except one . . . but the way these things are blended is the cause for long arguments and comparisons and even amicable differences among old friends.

Some insist that the oysters should be sizzled in the butter until they are curled, and then added to the hot milk. Others say they should be heated to boiling in their own juice, and that the boiling milk and the butter should be poured over them. Others say . . . But here is a sample of the variety of recipes that families and cookbooks have produced:

Oyster Stew[1]

1 *quart oysters*	4 *tablespoons butter*
2 *cups oyster liquor*	*celery salt*
2 *cups heavy cream*	*pepper*

Bring 1 cup of the oyster liquor to a boil and when it has cooked for 5 minutes skim off the top, which will be foamy. Add the cream, butter, and seasoning to taste. Cook the oysters in the other cup of liquor until the edges curl (about 5 minutes), strain and add to the cream. Serve immediately.

The use of celery salt in this recipe is probably less a regional custom than a trick used by one enthusiastic family for so long that it can almost be called "New England" now. It is like the odd but excellent amount of paprika slapped into the next rule by the energetic Browns in their *Country Cook Book*:

Oyster Stew[2]

Rinse a stewpan and put it on the fire without drying, so the milk won't stick. Dump in 1 quart of milk and 1 dozen oysters with their liquor and plenty of salt. Cook very slowly, without boiling of course, and give an occasional light stir to see how the oysters are plumping out. Just before their edges begin to curl, dump in ⅛ pound of sweet butter and at least 2 tablespoons of paprika. More paprika won't hurt, but will give a richer hue to the stew, and make you wish you'd made twice as much. Swirl the paprika and melted butter around to make an attractive, mottled topping and dish it out the second the edges begin to curl. If cooked any longer, the oysters will be hard.

[1]*New England Cook Book*, Culinary Arts Press, Reading, Pennsylvania, 1936.
[2]*Brown's Country Cook Book*, Farrar and Rinehart, New York, 1937.

The only stew I ever heard of made without either cream or milk, was from three gentle sisters. They spoke sadly at first, and then with that kind of quiet inner mirth that rises always in members of a family who have lived together for several decades, when they begin unexpectedly to remember things. These three sisters sat in the hot California light under a eucalyptus tree, and laughed at last in spite of all the things in between, as they recalled the way they always ate oyster stew when they were children in New Hampshire.

It was a strange stew, and could not have been as handsome as one made with cream, but it was even better, the sisters murmured with politeness but a kind of stubborn sensuality. It had a stronger, finer smell, they said . . . and it tasted purer, more completely *oyster*.

Their mother melted a good nubbin of fresh butter in a pan. In another pan she put the oysters, a dozen or so for everyone, with all their juices and about a cupful more of water for each dozen. She brought the water with the oysters in it just to the boil, so that the oysters began to think of curling without really getting at it, and then quickly skimmed them off and into a hot tureen. She brought the water to the boil again, and threw in pepper and salt. Then she poured the hot butter over the oysters, and the hot broth over all, and the three sisters and their other sisters and brothers and grandparents ate it steaming from the tureen, with butter crackers.

And here is a recipe for butter crackers, probably much like the ones eaten, those Sunday nights long ago, by the three gentle sisters. It is from *Common Sense in the Household*,[3] and is as far from packaged U-No-Snaps and all our cellophaned conformity as 1870 is from blitzkriegs:

[3]By Marion Harland, Scribner Armstrong and Company, New York, 1873.

Butter Crackers

1 *quart of flour*	1 *saltspoonful salt*
3 *tablespoonfuls butter*	2 *cups sweet milk*
½ *teaspoon soda, dissolved in*	
hot water	

Rub the butter into the flour, or, what is better, cut it up with a knife or chopper, as you do in pastry; add the salt, milk, soda, mixing well. Work into a ball, lay upon a floured board, and beat with the rolling-pin half an hour, turning and shifting the mass often. Roll into an even sheet, a quarter of an inch thick, or less, prick deeply with a fork, and bake hard in a moderate oven. Hang them up in a muslin bag in the kitchen for two days to dry.

(This is something you will probably never taste in your life, unless you are stubborn or have a crazy cook, but it is nice to know that there still live people who have eaten something other than the light dead things we call oyster crackers with their stews.)

Probably the best stew I ever ate was at the Doylestown Inn. It may have been so good because I was escaped from a long ride, cold enough to make my eyeballs hurt. Maybe it was because I was pleased by the narrow dark room and the Dutch farmers sitting quietly at the bar and the smell of the place, clean and masculine. I was happy to be there for those reasons and because I had long waited for the day, eager from tales I had heard. So the stew tasted better than any I had ever eaten, because of all that and because it was so good anyway.

It was made in three copper saucepans, as I remember, by a thin young-old man who said nonchalantly that oyster stews in Dublin were pretty good too, but couldn't touch his, of course. He strolled up and down the narrow gangplank behind the counter, and talked and put a platter of crackers and a hideous glass shaker of dark sherry in front of me, and all the time kept his eyes on the three pans, shaking them and pouring as he went.

In the smallest he put some butter from a big cool pat, and let it froth up once and then rest at the back of the stove. In the next he put oysters, fresh from their shells which he tossed into a bin under the counter. In the third, which was deeper and more a real saucepan than a kind of skillet, like the others, he put about a pint of milk and let it heat until it shivered on top. He kept his eye sharply on all three, so that the butter and the oysters and the milk never got beyond him.

As soon as the butter had frothed and settled he poured it quickly over the oysters and started skimming them around and around in the pan, like an old woman making an omelette at Mont Saint-Michel. In about one minute, not three or even five as so many recipes will say, he whiffed them past his questioning nose and then into the hot milk, which was just on the point of steaming. He put in red pepper and salt in a flash, and before I realized it the oyster stew I had so long talked about and waited for was under my own nose, and the young-old man stood watching me.

I sat for a minute, letting my eyeballs come into focus again and smelling the fine straightforward smell of the stew, and he got impatient and flicked a few drops of sherry into my plate, hinting that I get down to business. I did. It was as good as he had said, the best in the world, and as all the other people had told me . . . mildly potent, quietly sustaining, warm as love and welcomer in winter.

Like most people, though, who have ever tasted oyster stew in their first years, I still think the kind we used to make on Sunday nights when I was little was the kind I might make myself if I wanted one again . . . which I often do.

Now I am older, and I know that good stews can be made as

we made them then, but with tinned Willapoint oysters and store butter and bought milk. In spite of this knowledge, less my choice than a compromise with progress, I like to think of those first stews as the perfect ones, the dream stews.

The oysters were Chincoteagues . . . or would be if I were little again and in my dream at the same time . . . Chincoteagues alive and fluttering their gills minutely as they felt the air about them. They were dropped, clean and fat, into the heating milk . . . and the milk was not pasteurized and flat, nor was it homogenized and thick and "good for you," but it was whole milk from a cow half-Jersey and half-Guernsey. Just before the milk with the oysters in it began to steam, a few chunks of sweet saltless butter were put on the top, and salt and pepper, so that as the stew was poured into the hot tureen (a sturdy oval pot of white bone-china with a fat gold band around it) the butter and the condiments poured too, and mixed themselves evenly with the milk.

By then the oysters had grown even plumper, and were heated through but still tender. It was a fine stew, and we ate hot buttered toast with it. The toast is perhaps easier to duplicate now, but my memory of both is fine and reassuring, and "will do . . . for a supper to sleep on."

R is for Oyster

C. PEARL SWALLOW
He died of a bad oyster.

That is carved on a tombstone in a graveyard in Maine—Paris Hill, I think the place is called. The man's name was good for such an end, but probably the end was not.

If Mr. Swallow really died of a bad oyster he was a most miserable man for some hours, certainly. The bad oyster itself was rotten to his taste, so that he knew as soon as he had eaten it that he was wrong. Perhaps he worried a little about it, and then forgot and ate other things to rub the coppery taste from his tongue. He may, even in Maine, have washed it down with drink.

In two or five or six hours, though, he remembered. He felt faint, and cold fingers whuddered over his skin, so that he reeled and shivered. Then he was sick, violently and often. He could barely lift his head, for the weakness and the dreadful cramps in his belly. His bowels surged, so that he felt they would drain his very heart out of him. And, God, he was thirsty, thirsty. . . . I'm dying, he thought, and even in his woe he regretted it, and did not believe it. But he died.

Perhaps he died of a bad oyster. Oysters can be bad, all right, if they are stale and full of bacteria that make for putrefaction. Mushrooms can be deadly, too. But mushrooms and oysters are alike in that they take the blame, because of superstition and something innately mysterious about their way of life, for countless pains that never are their fault.

It is true that people have died from eating mushrooms, because there are at least two deadly ones and innocently or not, men have been fed them. It is true, too, that some men have eaten rotten oysters and died, hideously, racked with vomiting.

But quite often, I feel sure, mushrooms and oysters too are blamed for sickness that could equally be caused by many things like piggishness or nerves or even other poisons.

What man knowingly would eat a bad oyster, anyway? A bad oyster looks old and disagreeable in its shell, and it smells somewhat of copper and somewhat of rotten eggs. Of course, it might be hidden in a pie or a patty or under a coating of rich spiced sauce in a restaurant. But even so, a man's tongue would warn him that something was very wrong, I think, unless he was half under the table he sat at.

(In this, the oyster is kinder than the mushroom, which can taste most delicious when it is most deadly. And that is seldom, I insist.)

And in case a man's tongue warns him that he has at last swallowed that gastronomical rarity, a bad 'un, he should leave the board at once and do what men have always known how to do, even the dainty ones, and get rid of it.

There would be no mistaking it, once on the tongue. When people say, "I must have eaten a bad oyster yesterday . . . I've felt a bit dauncy ever since!" you can be sure that they have eaten a great many other things, and have perhaps drunk over well, but that they certainly have not swallowed what is so easy to blame. If so, they would have known the unpleasant truth immediately, because it would taste so thoroughly nasty . . . and of course within six hours or less they would have been sick as hell, or even dead.

Probably more people eat oysters now than ever before, because it is easier than ever to ship them from their beds and bottoms to the dining tables of this nation and any other nation whose people still have time for such things.

The old-fashioned habit of sniffing each oyster more or less delicately before swallowing it is as nearly extinct as its contemporary trick of gulping, with an all but visible holding of the nose, which was considered genteel . . . and *so* much safer.

Restaurants, even air-cooled perforce in the midst of hot sand, like Palm Springs, or as far from the sea as Oskaloosa in Iowa, can serve oysters without fear these days. Tycoons with inlets in Maryland have their highfalutin molluscs flown for supper that night to a penthouse in Fort Worth, or to a simple log-cabin Away from It All in the Michigan woods, and know that Space and Time and even the development of putrescent bacteria stand still for dollars. Bindlestiffs on a rare bender in Los Angeles (Ell-ay, you say) gulp down three swollen "on the half's" with a rot gut whiskey chaser in any of a dozen joints on Main Street, and are more than moderately sure that if they die that night, it won't be from the oysters.

Men's ideas, though, continue to run in the old channels about oysters as well as God and war and women. Even when they know better they insist that months with *R* in them are all right, but that oysters in June or July or May or August will kill you or make you wish they had. This is wrong, of course, except that all oysters, like all men, are somewhat weaker after they have done their best at reproducing.

Several decades ago, a jolly man wrote:

> "Let's sing a song of glory to Themistocles O'Shea
> Who ate a dozen oysters on the second
> Day of May . . ."

And even the government tells us *R*'s are silly. "A clean fat oyster may be eaten with impunity at any time of the year," the officials say in folder after folder.

Doctors tell us so. "Hell, if it smells good, it's okay," they say, with modifications dictated by their practices and their positions in the Association.

Men who write pamphlets called *Hypochlorite process of oyster purification, report on experimental purification of polluted oysters, on commercial scale, by floating them in sea water treated with hyperchloride of calcium. (Public Health Reprint 652.) . . 5 . . T27 . 6/a: 652* say so, as do earnest Japanese who deliver papers before the Kokusai Yorei Kabushiki Kaisha called *Kaki no banasi*, which means *Talk on Oysters*, with surprisingly un-Oriental bluntness.

They all say that oysters are all right any time as long as they are healthy . . . all, that is, except the oyster-farmers.

The farmers' actions are understandable, after all. Their main interest is in growing as many good crops as they can, and it stands to reason that if a healthy female, round with some twenty million eggs, is taken from the water before she has a chance to birth them, the farmers lose.

May and June and July, and of course August, are the months when the waters are warmest almost everywhere along the coasts, and it is remarkably convenient that oysters can only breed their spawn when the temperature is around seventy degrees and in months with no *R*'s in them. How easy it has been to build a catchy gastronomic rule on the farmers' interest in better crops!

People who have broken the rule and been able to buy oysters in the forbidden months say that they are most delicious then, full and flavorsome. They should be served colder than in winter, and eaten at the far end of a stifling day, in an almost empty chophouse, with a thin cold Alsatian wine to float them down

. . . and with them disappear the taste of carbon dioxide and sweaty clerks from the streets outside, so that even July in a big city seems for a time to be a most beautiful month, and C. Pearl Swallow's ghost well-laid.

The Well-Dressed Oyster

Any man may be in good spirits and good temper when he's
well dressed. There ain't much credit in that.
Martin Chuzzlewit, CHARLES DICKENS

There are three kinds of oyster-eaters: those loose-minded
sports who will eat anything, hot, cold, thin, thick, dead or
alive, as long as it is *oyster*; those who will eat them raw and only
raw; and those who with equal severity will eat them cooked
and no way other.

The first group may perhaps have the most fun, although
there is a white fire about the others' bigotry that can never
warm the broad-minded.

There is a great deal to be said in favor of the second group,
for almost every oyster-eater who does not belong whole-
heartedly to the third and last division, would die before deny-
ing that a perfect oyster, healthy, of fine flavor, plucked from its
chill bed and brought to the plate unwatered and unseasoned, is
more delicious than any of its modifications. On the other
hand, a flaccid, moping, debauched mollusc, tired from too
much love and loose-nerved from general world conditions,
can be a shameful thing served raw upon its shell.

It is then that the third group, the fanatical believers in the
power of heat and sauces to hide a multitude of real or imagined

evils, comes triumphantly into its own. Any oyster, even a tinned steamed Japanese bastard from the coast of Oregon can be in good spirits and good temper when he's well dressed, they say. And they are right.

That is unfortunate, if you distrust the saw that what you don't know can't hurt you, for in that case any cooked oyster is suspect, and good old-fashioned ptomaine leers behind every casserole and chafing dish.

It is fortunate, in that the inventing of disguises has brought forth a wealth of subtle ingenious recipes, rather as fast-days in the Middle Ages forced the church's greatest minds to invent ways to make eggs and cheese taste like roast veal. Some of the recipes for cooking oysters are simple, and no less good, and some of them are as insanely elaborate as the jaded bilious gourmets who gave birth to them.

One of the best and easiest dishes that can be made, if you like it, is baked oysters, and this is as good a recipe as any, whether you call it baked or scalloped or *en casserole* or what:

Baked Oysters

Into a shallow baking dish, well buttered, spread a light layer of bread or cracker crumbs. Then put in a layer of oysters, and season well with salt and fresh ground pepper and bits of sweet butter. Then put more crumbs and alternate in this fashion until the dish is almost full, and put crumbs and butter on top. Pour enough oyster juice to moisten things, and bake in a quick oven until brown but not bubbling.

Variations can be played *ad infinitum* on this theme, even by beginners and harried hurriers, and sliced onions, tomato sauce, herbs, mustard, cream all find a fairly safe resting-place in it.

Probably the next simplest way to cook an oyster, and the one most commonly accepted in restaurants, is to fry him. It is too bad, since the method can be good, that so many chefs dip their oysters in a thick and often infamous batter, which at once plunged into the equally obscene grease, forms an envelope of such slippery toughness that the oyster within it lies helpless and steaming in a foul blanket, tasteless and yet powerfully indigestible.

Firm chilled oysters rolled quickly in crumbs and dipped into good fat for almost no time at all, and then served quickly on hot plates with an honest tartar sauce or lemon slices, can be one of the best dishes anywhere, and it is perhaps a proof that optimism is inherently human and that after several hideous experiences with restaurant-fried oysters, I still say it.

A good tartar sauce can be bought in a bottle, like several other things, but a better one can be made from this recipe, which is easy if you have an herb garden, and impossible, but still fun to think about, if you do not:

Tartar Sauce[1]

1 *cup mayonnaise*	1 *teaspoon capers*
1 *teaspoon chopped chives*	*dash cayenne*
1 *teaspoon tarragon*	1 *chopped olive*
1 *teaspoon chervil*	*prepared mustard to taste*
1 *chopped gherkin*	*(optional)*
	wine vinegar to taste

Mix all ingredients except vinegar, then put that in slowly until the proper tartness is obtained. Approximately 1 tablespoon will be necessary.

As soon as oysters leave the relatively safe confines of butter-and-seasoning, the sky, illimitable, is the limit, and man's inventive genius plays one wild trick after another. In spite of all

[1]*Herbs for the Kitchen*, Irma Goodrich Mazza, Little, Brown and Company, Boston, 1940.

the zany recipes, however, many are good, if somewhat too elaborate, and the oyster usually emerges from them in spite of all its trappings.

It is pleasant, now and then, to make a good mushroom and cream sauce, mix oysters in it, and put the whole in ramekins, with crumbs on top, for a hot minute or two.

Or, hardly fancier, this Louisiana recipe for a gumbo (without okra, oddly enough for such a local dish) is easy to make and very good, and the saffron in it makes you think of bouillabaisse in Marseille, or of risotto under the glass arcade at Biffi's in Milano:

Oyster Gumbo

⅔	cup finely diced onion	2	dozen oysters
2	tablespoons butter or good olive oil	1½	cups water
4	tablespoons flour	3	tablespoons finely cut parsley
2	bay leaves	1½	to 3 teaspoons powdered saffron, according to taste
1	teaspoon salt		
5	drops Evangeline (or tabasco) sauce		

Sauté the onion in butter in a heavy pan or casserole until limp but not brown. Blend in flour and bay, salt, and tabasco.

Drain the oysters, saving the liquor, and add liquor and water gradually to the mixture, stirring well. Cook about fifteen minutes, stirring now and then.

Add the oysters, parsley, and saffron, and stir well. Serve as soon as steaming, in a bowl with a dish of fluffy hot rice beside it. Ladle onto the rice on generous dinner-plates.

Or, in natural progression toward the baroque and away from simple things, this recipe from *Fit for a King*[2] is good, in spite of

[2]Merle Armitage, Longmans, Green and Company, New York, 1939.

its little dibbles and dashes of this and that . . . and it is given by Roy Alciatore, the slender-faced son of the house of Antoine, in New Orleans, which should make it triply worthy (and also explain how so many sauces could be assembled for one little dish):

Oysters à la Foch

Spread a piece of toast lightly with sausage meat and cook under a salamander. Fry ½ dozen oysters and place on toast. With ¾ Espagnal and ¼ tomato make a sauce to which you will add a spoonful of Hollandaise sauce, a dash of Lea and Perrins sauce and a dash of sherry wine. Mix well together and pour over the oysters on toast. Serve.

Far removed as this recipe may seem from the ordinary kitchen's possibilities, it still has not that fabulous quality of the rule quoted by everyone from Richelieu's chef to Crosby Gaige, in which you put one thing inside another until you have something more or less the size of an elephant, then roast the whole, and finally throw away all but the innermost thing. For instance, you start with an oyster. You put it inside a large olive. then you put the olive inside an ortolan (a wee bird called "the garden bunting," in case you are among the underprivileged), and the ortolan inside a lark, and so on and so on. In the end, you have a roasted oyster. Or perhaps a social revolution.

Probably the most rabble-rousing recipe I ever heard, if the rabble could have listened, was one told me under the table, so to speak, by a cadaverous old man who had reigned at various times in the kitchens of all the crowned heads and banker-princes of *fin-de-Hapsbourg* Europe. He was a Russian, as far as could be known, and when I met him he was running a little box near Toulon in France, the kind frequented by Turkish and

Egyptian millionaires who gave him three days' warning and came in twelve Rolls-Royces, and he was living solely on American gin and bicarbonate of soda.

He felt toward gastronomy as some men feel toward beautiful terrible women, and his conversation was for the most part a series of diatribes and scurrilous anecdotes about dishes he had made, much as most lecherous old men's leering reminiscences would be about girls they had done the same thing to.

His recipe for "Oysters à la Bazeine," as far as it can be cleared of his multilingual obscenities, is as follows, and is obviously not recommended to the bride of three weeks who just loves to stir up pretty dishes in her kitchenette:

Oysters à la Bazeine
(or Honi Soit Qui Mal Y Pense)

Have on hand adequate supplies of sauce Béchamel, sauce Soubise, *and* velouté. *(Recipes can be found in Escoffier's* Guide Culinaire, *in Dumas's* Grand Dictionnaire de Cuisine, *or even in André Simon's* French Cook Book.*)*

Prepare a roux of chopped chives, butter, and rice-flour, and set it aside.

Slice truffles paper-thin, and cut into the shapes of dolphins, crabs, and other sea-monsters. Set them aside.

Poach brook trout, preferably alive, in a court bouillon made with a good dry champagne instead of oridinary wine and water. Set them aside.

Make a marinade, using fine *instead of wine-vinegar, and in it marinate small cubes of Parma ham for several hours, or until a faint iridescence appears. Drain, and set aside.*

Prepare croutes *by browning thick slices of fine white bread in Strasbourg goose-fat, and do not set aside.*

Instead, place them quickly on heated plates. Spread each tranche *with* Béchamel *and then the roux. Set a trout carefully upon it, and coat with* Soubise. *Over this sprinkle the cubes of Parma ham, and then a thin layer of* velouté. *Decorate lavishly with the truffle-silhouettes, and serve at once under bells with a modest but well-bred Sainte-Croix du Château Pinardino '08.*

Or fry oysters and serve with ale.

Take 300 Clean Oysters

Oysters are the usual opening to a winter breakfast . . .
indeed they are almost indispensable.
Almanach des Gourmands, 1803

For hundreds of years men have ascribed all kinds of potent qualities to oysters, aphrodisiac and more purely practical. For one, they are supposed to be good for you.

Resturants and bars and even governments bring out various attractive kinds of propaganda, which tell in a thousand ways why you should eat the molluscs that in spite of publicity have been a favorite food for thousands and thousands of years.

Oysters are healthful and nourishing, full of all the chemical elements such as oxygen, hydrogen, nitrogen, and on and on, which occur regularly in your own body and are necessary to it. They keep you fit, do oysters, with vitamins and such, for energy and what is lightly called "fuel value." They prevent goiter. They build up your teeth. They keep your children's legs straight, and when Junior reaches puberty they make his skin clear and beautiful as a soap-opera announcer's dream. They add years to your life . . .

And . . .

They contain more phosphorus than any other food!

Phosphorus is a brain food, the most important one, according to popular belief for centuries and publicity men for oyster companies and even a few reputable scientists. It has been called that for a long time: Cicero ate oysters to nourish his eloquence, and the ancients used them with a startlingly cold-blooded combination of gastronomy and pure hygiene.

Long before the fifteenth century of our era, people ate them and other fish to aid their intellects. Somewhere after 1461, indeed, Louis XI made it obligatory, at least for the group of great men he gathered to him in his fabulous reign, to swallow a certain amount of such easy phosphorus each day.

The king's physicians ruled him as thoroughly as he ruled the Scots and Italians and Portuguese in his councils, and since Louis ate oysters by prescription, so did all influential France, less from choice than from political wisdom. And the professors of the Sorbonne, the real wise men of France, could not even pretend that politics entered into their diet.

Professors, Louis reasoned, should be as intelligent as possible, since they represented him, "le roi terrible," and therefore he saw that they did not disappoint him. Once a year, willy-nilly, they were served a dinner at the king's orders, and at that dinner they were bound to eat, and eat prodigiously, of oysters. It was to make them bright, and once accomplished, keep them so!

A little later, in the times of Voltaire and Pope and Swift, oysters were considered less a food than as an *apéritif*, so that it was quite usual to serve ten or twelve dozen to each guest as a "starter" for a banquet. An old recipe begins: "Take 300 clean oysters and throw into a pot filled with nice butter . . ." One man, old Marshal Turgot, who knew almost too much about famines, was able in fatter days to eat a hundred oysters before breakfast just to whet his appetite.

And when the infamous Whistling Oyster of Drury Lane

started his daily pipings on the pub-bar (which kept up for a suspiciously long time when you consider the seasonal existence of such shellfish), and drew enormous hungry crowds of delighted listeners, oyster-eating became a necessity not only to the snobs but to the common people, not to mention the bourgeoisie.

Since then, really, almost any Western man with a few cents in his pocket and a little time on his hands can swallow a certain amount of phosphorus, and it is still good as long as the oysters are fresh and clean, whether it goes to nourish his brain, his belly, or his most private parts.

A Lusty Bit
of Nourishment

Cook, white, must understand oysters. Apply aft. 1 p.m.
Iliffe, 847 E. Allegheny.

Advertisement in *Philadelphia Inquirer,*
March 1941

The flavor of an oyster depends upon several things. First, if it
is fresh and sweet and healthy it will taste good, quite simply
. . . good, that is, if the taster like oyster.

Then, it will taste like a Chincoteague or a blue point or a mild
oyster from the Louisiana bayous or perhaps a metallic tiny
Olympia from the Western coast. Or it may have a clear harsh
flavor, straight from a stall in a wintry French town, a stall piled
herringbone style with Portugaises and Garennes, green as
death to the uninitiated and twice as toothsome. Or it may taste
firm and yet fat, like the English oysters from around Plym-
outh.

Then an oyster will taste like what the taster expects, which
of course depends entirely on the taster. Myself, since I was sev-
enteen I have expected all oysters to be delicious, and with few
exceptions they have been. In the same way, some people wait,

if they manage to swallow these shellfish at all, to gag more or less violently. And they gag.

Oysters can be eaten for themselves, as on the half shell or even in cooked dishes; they can be eaten primarily for the sauce that coats them, as in Oysters à la Rockefeller and all their offspring; and they can be eaten as a flavoring . . . oyster stuffing, for example.

Oyster stuffing, for turkeys naturally, is as American as corn-on-the-cob or steamed coot, as far as Americans know or care. To many families it is a necessary part of Christmas dinner, so that its omission would at once connotate a sure sign of internal disintegration, as if Ma came to church in her corset-cover or Uncle Jim brought his light-o'-love to the children's picnic.

It would mean financial failure too, to leave out those oysters that not so long ago were brought carefully a thousand miles for the fortunate moneybags in Iowa and Missouri who could boast of them in their holiday stuffings. Not every man could buy them, God knows, even if he wanted to, and a middle westerner was even prouder than a man from Down East to have these shellfish on his feast-day.

Perhaps it is because they were somewhat lacking in their first freshness by the time they reached Peoria; perhaps it was because the people of this land so far from seashores were abashed by shells: whatever the reason, oysters in the Middle West were always cooked . . . and still are, mostly. And in spite of evidence, turkey stuffing seems primarily a part of that cookery. In it, oysters are used for their flavor, quite simply.

There are many recipes, from New England cookbooks as well as those spotted brown pamphlets issued yearly by the Ladies' Aids and Guild Societies of small towns beyond the Mississippi. All of them agree that it is almost impossible to put too many oysters in a turkey dressing if you are going to put in any at all.

The method of using them differs, of course, so that one rule will say, "Mince ½ dozen thoroughly and sprinkle throughout the crumbs," and another will command more generously, "Fill cavity of bird with large plump blue points." A fair medium, however, is the following recipe from Mrs. William Vaughn Moody's *Cook Book:*[1]

Dressing for Turkey or Other Fowl with Oysters

1 ½ *quarts of fine counts*	1 *quart of oyster juice*
1 *quart of lightly fried crumbs*	*salt, pepper, celery salt, and paprika*

Wing the oysters. Add the bread crumbs, oyster juice, and seasoning.

I would add, with the Browns in their *Country Cook Book*, that "Perhaps Oyster stuffing is one of the best, but the crumbs, which are mixed with the oysters and oyster liquor, should be literally soaked in melted butter, as should all crumbs that go into a turkey." For myself, I also like a cup or more of finely chopped celery stirred in with the crumbs, rather than Mrs. Moody's celery salt.

There is a recipe in the book Merle Armitage and his wife cooked up called *Fit for a King* that is less conventional, but very good for those who don't want any nonsense about hiding the oysters. It is called, simply enough,

Oyster Stuffing

Toast some thin slices of bread until brown and butter them. Lay 2 slices flat inside the turkey and over them put a good layer of raw oysters seasoned with salt and pepper, lemon juice, and a few pieces of butter. Over

[1]Charles Scribner's Sons, New York, 1931.

this lay two more slices of toast and then a layer of oysters as before. The resulting flavor is delicious.

Between these two recipes there are ten thousand variations, probably, but the general idea of using oysters as a flavoring is no new one to us, any more than it has been for some several thousand years to the Chinese.

They probably are the longest users of these molluscs in such fashion. It has been going on for centuries, like so many other quaint Oriental customs, so that the oldest cookbooks give practically the same recipes used today in Hong Kong and the kitchens of bewildered blonde brides in other outposts-of-Empire.

There are two kinds of oysters used in Chinese cooking for their flavor. There is *ho tsee*, the dried oyster, and then there is *ho yeou*, which is so much like our old-fashioned oyster catsup that I wonder if it was not brought back to us by one of those doughty old sea captains whose spirits still search for the Northwest Passage far past Java Head.

Marion Harland's 1873 edition of *Common Sense in the House-hold* gives a recipe that is probably as good as any outside a Chinese grocery, although other more modern cookbooks are less bound by tee-totalitarianism than she, and more willing to forgo vinegar altogether and put in a full quart of sherry for each quart of shellfish. Here is Mrs. Harland's recipe:

Oyster Catsup

1 *quart oysters*	1 *tablespoon salt*
1 *teacupful cider vinegar*	1 *teaspoon cayenne pepper,*
1 *teacupful sherry*	*and same of mace*

Chop the oysters and boil in their own liquor with a teacupful vinegar, skimming the scum as it rises. [It is here that such devil-may-care moderns as the Browns in their *Country Cook Book* say, "To each pint of oysters add a pint of sherry, let come to a boil . . ."] *Boil three minutes, strain through a hair-cloth, return the liquor to the fire, add the wine, pepper, salt, and mace. Boil fifteen minutes, and when cold, bottle for use, sealing the corks.*

Mr. Henry Low, who is an authority on Chinese food, says of a *ho yeou* which might as well be Mrs. Harland's, for all the difference we could know, "Very delicious to serve with cold boiled chicken." In spite of the somewhat Charlie Chan-ish swing to this sentence, the opinion is a good one.

So is his inclusion, in *Cook at Home in Chinese,*[2] of at least one recipe using dried oysters, which can be bought at almost any Oriental grocery store in this country and are very much like the smoked oysters people give you now at cocktail parties, excellent little shriveled things on toothpicks which make your mouth taste hideous unless you drink a lot, which may also make your mouth taste hideous. Probably our smoked oysters could be used as well as *ho tsee*, but I doubt if they should be soaked. Or perhaps I am mistaken.

Anyway, here is Mr. Low's recipe for

Dried Oysters with Vegetables
(Ho Tsee Soong)

½ *pound dried oysters* (ho tsee)
1 *cup chopped bamboo shoots* (jook tsun)
1 *cup chopped Chinese cabbage* (bok choy)
1 *cup peeled chopped water chestnuts* (ma tai)

2 *tablespoons oyster sauce* (ho yeou)
½ *teaspoon sugar*
½ *cup water*
a pinch of salt
a dash of pepper

[2] The Macmillan Company, New York, 1938.

½ cup chopped raw lean pork
1 clove crushed garlic
1 piece crushed green ginger

½ head shredded Boston lettuce
1 teaspoon gourmet powder
   (mei jing)
2 teaspoons cornstarch

Soak oysters five hours and cut off hard parts. Chop fine. Mix together all chopped ingredients, add ginger, garlic, gourmet powder, salt, pepper and sugar. Put in a hot, well-greased skillet and cook four minutes. Add oyster sauce and water and cook four minutes more. Add cornstarch, which has been made into a smooth paste. Stir, and cook one minute. Arrange lettuce leaves on platter and pour cooked mixture over them.

It is not such a far cry as it seems from the exotic blendings of this Ho Tsee Soong to the pungency of Oysters à la Rockefeller. Both dishes depend almost more upon the herbs that make up their body than they do upon the oysters that are the raison d'être, and whether they are "dry and putrid" in a dark kitchen in Chungking or San Francisco, or fresh in New Orleans, the herbs must be prepared with finicky attention.

There are too many legends, really, about Oysters Rockefeller for any one to dare say what he thinks is the true one. It is equally foolish to say what is the true recipe since every gourmet who has ever dined in that nostalgically agreeable room of Antoine's on St. Louis Street figures, after the third or fourth sampling if not the first, that he has at last discovered the secret.

It is true that Mr. Alciatore, like his father and grandfather, has managed to keep his Rockefellers consistently delicious. That is perhaps the reason why they are so justly famous, rather than any special secret formula. Other restaurants serve their own versions, which may be a little cheaper or even a little more expensive, and may look almost like Antoine's. But they are undependable, so that sometimes the rock salt they rest on is half an inch thick and sometimes an inch; sometimes the covering, that little soft green blanket over each oyster, is dark, and sometimes it is lightly mottled, with logical differences in the flavor of the dish itself.

(This simple, apparently difficult secret for success has also been copied by the barmen in the Roosevelt Hotel in New Orleans, too: unchanging excellence. According to their publicity, they are the only makers of the Original Ramos Gin Fizz, that subtle smooth-like drink that has nourished reporters and politicians and other humans through many a long foodless summer near the simmering bayous.

(Once, for reasons of research, I drank two Ramos fizzes away from the hallowed Roosevelt. They were truly bad. I went back to the hotel, and watched eagerly while the old barman put little dashes of this and that together and then handed it all to the strong young stevedore who was chief shaker. I decided that infinite care, unhurried patience, and a never varying formula were more the secret than any magic element such as dried nectar-crumbs or drops from a Ramos philter.

(I proved this theory, at least to my pleasure, when with infinite care and a certain amount of unhurried patience I too made a Ramos, after a recipe I found that was printed in 1900 for Solari's Grocery. It was easy to assemble, once I located some orange-flower water . . . and it was, Heaven protect me for this blasphemy!, as good as any ever shook up at the Roosevelt.)

Oysters Rockefeller, then, surrounded as they are by pomp and legend, are not impossible to copy. Their miracle is that *chez* Antoine, where the last two Alciatores have served them ever since 1889, they have always been delicious. Probably it is safe to say that they have not varied one jot or tittle in all these years, so that Mr. Roy could feel quite safe in sitting down to the millionth order, complete with photographers and headwaiter-with-wine-basket, to dip into the first succulent shell with only a faint sign of suspicion on his small intelligent face.

The postcards resulting from this occasion are given to every person who eats Oysters à la Rockefeller at Antoine's, and on each one, like the number of your duck in the old days at the Tour d'Argent in Paris (Where else?), is stamped the number of your plate of these famous morsels. It is an endearing bit of chi-chi, which is barely marred by the italics under the picture: *The recipe is a sacred family secret.*

That is rather more than chi-chi, although equally endearing in its solemnity. It is what could be called an exaggeration of truth, since, although the Alciatores may use three-quarters of a teaspoon of this or that rather than a half, there are many private cooks who have a recipe that is as good, Louisiana gourmets say, as Antoine's own.

This is it, reprinted from *A Book of Famous Old New Orleans Recipes Used in the South for More Than Two Hundred Years*:

Oysters Rockefeller

Procure oysters on the half shell, wash them and drain them, and put them back on the shells. Place ice cream salt to the thickness of about one half inch on a platter and preheat, placing the oysters that are on the half shells on the hot salt and run them in the broiler for five minutes. Then cover with the following sauce and bread crumbs and bake in the hot oven until brown. Serve hot.

Sauce for Oysters Rockefeller

1 cup oyster water	1 ounce herbsaint
1 cup plain water	1 cup best butter
¼ bunch shallots	¼ bunch spinach
1 small sprig thyme	1 tablespoon Worcestershire
½ cup ground bread crumbs	sauce
toasted and sifted	2 small stalks green celery

Grind all the vegetables in the chopper. Put the water and the oyster li-
quor together, and let boil vigorously for about five minutes, then add
the ground vegetables and cook about twenty minutes or until it's to the
consistency of a thick sauce.

Stir in the butter until melted and remove from fire, add the herb-
saint, pour sauce over oysters on the shells, sprinkle with bread crumbs,
return to hot oven for five minutes and serve piping hot on the platter in
which you cooked them.

(Herbsaint is a cordial made in the deep South from various
herbs but mostly anise, so that it tastes very much like that clear
Anis Mono that used to be served in Spanish pubs, or even like
Pernod. Some people say that Antoine's spurns it in Oysters
Rockefeller, but I wouldn't know. Myself, I think not.)

It is more than likely that if Mr. Alciatore, to say nothing of
his head chef, Camille Averna, should see this recipe he would
toss his head slightly, or perhaps even sneer. However, sacred
family secret or no, I still believe that any good cook with skill
and, above all, unfailing patience can make Oysters à la Rockefeller that are as like Antoine's as one angel can be like another.

The question is, Who wants to? Perhaps you are an habitué or
perhaps you have been to Antoine's once or twice. The inescap-
able charm of that simple, almost austere room, with mirrors
for walls; with the blue gas lamps flickering through all the evening while the electric lights snap on and off for the blazings of
crêpes Suzette and *cafés brûlots au diable*; with its high cashier's seat
at the back and its deft impersonal waiters who let the pantry
doors swing wide open now and then to show the ordered
shimmer of the wine-glass cupboard: all that makes a family secret much more precious than any recipe, and one that means
untellable pleasure to untold amateur gourmets.

Whether they are men like "the Grand Duke Alexis, brother
of the Czar of Russia," or Sinclair Lewis, or "Mr. Nobody
from Nowhere," they find at Antoine's something remem-

bered, something perhaps never known but recognized, so that dining there is full of ease and mellowness. *Huitres en Coquilles à la Rockefeller* appear magically, prepared with loving patience for each eager diner as if he were the first and only gastronome, and their tedious preparation is something that can best be left to Camille Averna's direction.

It should never matter that other people, armed with determination and an almost perfect copy of the Alciatores' recipe, could probably do just as well. Better go once to the little place on St. Louis Street in New Orleans, and eat them as they should be eaten, than struggle doggedly a thousand times with hot salt-beds and spinach-grindings in Connecticut or California. Oysters à la Rockefeller any place but *chez* Antoine are not quite as delicious, not quite as kosher nor as *comme il faut*.

There are, of course, at least ten other precious recipes for every thousand humans who have ever cooked an oyster. There are fairly complicated ones, like the following rule contributed to the first number of the magazine *Gourmet* by the Hotel Pierre of New York and its head chef, Georges Gonneau:

French Creamed Oysters

Put 1 cup of butter into the top of a lighted chafing-dish; add 1 tablespoon English mustard, ¼ teaspoon anchovy paste; salt, pepper, and a dash of cayenne pepper to taste; stir until mixture is thoroughly blended. Add 3 cups finely chopped celery and stir almost constantly until celery is nearly cooked. Pour in 1 quart rich, fresh cream slowly, stirring constantly until mixture comes to a boil. Add 4 dozen oysters, cleaned and free from beard, and 2 two minutes. Finally, add ¼ cup good sherry wine. Serve on freshly made toast on hot plates, and garnish with quartered lemon and crisp young watercress. Dust each serving with paprika, mixed with a little nutmeg.

This recipe, an excellent way to exercise man's basic fascination for chafing dishes and vice versa, is naturally much simpler than some, even though sautéed ham and mushrooms be added, or truffles; and on the other hand it is a great deal more elaborate than such a one as Marion Harland gave in 1870 and many years before.

She wrote with a passion which was always ladylike in spite of its perhaps ungenteel *gourmandise*, as her period dictated, but she was never squeamish, and her "receipts" are to a large number of aficionados as beautifully rounded as the Songs of Solomon. Witness what she said, so long ago and only yesterday, about

Roast Oysters

There is no pleasanter frolic for an Autumn evening, in the regions where oysters are plentiful, than an impromptu "roast" in the kitchen. There the oysters are hastily thrown into the fire by the peck. You may consider that your fastidious taste is marvelously respected if they are washed first. A bushel basket is set to receive the empty shells, and the click of the oyster-knives forms a constant accompaniment to the music of laughing voices. Nor are roast oysters amiss upon your own quiet supper-table, when the "good man" comes in on a wet night, tired and hungry, and wants "something heartening." Wash and wipe the shell-oysters, and lay them in the oven, if it is quick; upon the top of the stove, if it is not. When they are open, they are done. Pile in a large dish, and send to table. Remove the upper shells by a dexterous wrench of the knife, season the oyster on the lower, with pepper-sauce and butter, or pepper, salt, and vinegar in lieu of the sauce, and you have the very aroma of this pearl of bivalves, pure and undefiled.

Or [she adds, rather in anti-climax], *you may open while raw, leaving the oysters upon the lower shells; lay in a large baking-pan, and roast in their own liquor, adding pepper, salt, and butter before serving.*

Probably the "pepper sauce" used by Mrs. Harland's frolicking family was made more or less after this old New England recipe:

Roast Oyster Sauce

2 *tablespoons butter*	4 *drops tabasco sauce*
juice of 1 lemon	*juice of ½ onion*

Melt the butter, stir in the other ingredients and pour over oysters. Serve hot.

The Harland recipe is not much different from one given in *Plats du Jour*[3] by Paul Reboux, but its style is as much like his as his own flippant punning words are like the silence that comes now from his once garrulous land of wit and gaiety:

Grilled Oysters

. . . Surely, this recipe would not have the approval of the S.P.C.A. But it is probable that oysters possess a sensitivity analogous to that of the French tax-payer, so that they are incapable of very characteristic reactions. That, then, is why there is little reason for weeping tenderly at the idea that these molluscs must be placed on the grill.

As they submit to the same end that overtook Saint Lawrence, the oysters open. It is exactly like the purse of the government pensioner as Income Tax Day rolls around: one does the only possible thing in the presence of bad luck.

Take advantage of their being open to pop in a little melted butter, some pepper, and some bread crumbs. Then close them up again: at this moment they will be too weak to resist you. Let them cook a little. And serve them very hot.

Some people like this very much.

All oysters cooked in sauce, whether their own or manufactured, are necessarily of a certain complexity. They may be as simple as Marion Harland's or Reboux's; they may be coated with the intricacies of roux and white-wine sauces. They may even be surrounded by the strange legends of Antoine's, so that

[3]Flammarion, Paris, 1936.

their consumption becomes more a rite than the simple manifestation of a hunger.

According to the little black-and-gold booklet published for Antoine's centennial, Oysters à la Rockefeller contain "such rich ingredients that the name of the Multi-Millionaire was borrowed to indicate their value." Some gourmets say that any oyster worthy of its species should not be toyed with and adulterated by such skullduggeries as this sauce of herbs and strange liqueurs. Others, more lenient, say that Southern oysters like Mr. Alciatore's need some such refinement, being as they are languid and soft-tasting to the tongue.

They are, you might say, more like the Southern ladies than the brisk New Englanders. They are delicate and listless . . . and ice is scarce, or used to be . . . and the weather's no good for saving; best cover the bayou-molluscs with a fine New Orleans sauce, or at least a dash or two of red Evangeline. . . .

But further north, men choose their oysters without sauce. They like them cold, straightforward, simple, capable of spirit but unadorned, like a Low Church service maybe or a Boston romance.

And oysters of the North Atlantic Coast are worthy of this more or less unquestioning trust. They are firm and flavorful, and eaten chilled from their own lower shell with a bit of lemon juice squeezed over them they are among men's true delights.

There are, oddly enough, almost as many ways to eat such a simple dish as there are men to eat it.

First, several millennia ago, men cracked the shells and sucked out the tender gray bodies with their attendant juices and their inevitable sharp splinters. Then, when knives came, they pried open the two shells and cupped the lower one in their hands, careful not to spill its colorless elixer. And always, even from the beginning, there have been variations on these two simple processes; there has been invented a series of behavior-rules as complex as the recipes to prevent seasickness or how to arrange three tulips in a low jade-green bowl for the local garden show.

If a man cared, and knew all the rules, he would be really frightened to go into a decent oyster-bar and submit his knowledge to the cold eyes of the counterman and all the local addicts. He would be so haunted by what was correct in that certain neighborhood and how to hold the shell and whether the lemon juice should be used and so on that he would probably go instead to a corner drugstore and order a double chocolate banana-split.

Fortunately, though, almost everybody who goes into an oyster-bar or even eats in a restaurant is so pleased with the oysters themselves that he eats them in his own fashion without giving a toot or a tinkle about what other people think.

In America, on the East Coast, oysters are usually served on a plate of shaved ice, with small round white crackers in a bowl or vase. Quite often a commendable battery of bottled sauces such as tabasco and horseradish accompanies the order, and in many restaurants a little cup of red sauce with a tomato base is put in the middle of the plate of ice-and-oysters. Either this little cup of sauce or one of the bottles contains gastronomic heat in one form or another.

In New Orleans' oyster-bars, and all over the Western World in what used to be called "places of the people . . . common places," the procedure is simpler, almost as simple as the English pub-custom of shoving you your oysters, a toothpick to pluck them with, and a shaker of weak vinegar if you're toff enough to want it. Down South there is a long marble or hardwood counter between the customer and the oyster-man, sloping toward the latter. He stands there, opening the shells with a skill undreamed of by an ordinary man and yet always with a few cuts showing on his fingers, putting the open oysters carefully, automatically, on a slab of ice in front of him, while a cat waits with implacable patience at his ankles for a bit of oyster-beard or a caress. He throws the top shells behind him into a barrel, and probably they go into a road or a wall somewhere, later, with cement to bind them.

A man comes into the bare place, which has hard lights, and sawdust on the floor. He mutters "One" or "Two" to the oyster-man, and pulls a handful of square soda-crackers from the tipped glass jar at the end of the counter. If he wants to, he spoons out a cupful of tomato sauce from a big crock.

By then his one or two dozen oysters wait in a line for him upon the cold counter, their shells tipped carefully so that the liquor will lie still in them and not flow down the sloping marble and into the bins of unopened shells underneath. He picks up an oyster on a pointed thin little fork, and holds the shell under his chin while he guides it toward his mouth, having dunked it or not in the garish sauce, and then he swallows it.

If he likes raw oysters he enjoys this ceremony very much. Many do not, and may they long rest happy, if envious. Now, having wasted too many years in shuddering at oysters, I like them. I *thoroughly* like them, so that I am willing to forgo comfort and at times even safety to savor their strange cold succulence.

I was quite willing, once at the Old Port in Marseille before things changed, to risk their brassy greenness at a quayside stand. Once I knowingly ate a "bad one" in the Pompeiian Room at the Bern-Palace rather than cry them shame. And now, after more than a few years of prejudiced acquaintance, I can still say that oysters please me.

Those years, which have not been quite empty of perception, have made me form a few ideas of my own, since it is impossible to enjoy without thought, in spite of what the sensualists say.

I am still very ignorant, but I know that I used to like *Portu-*

gaises vertes and oysters from Garennes, in the times that seem so far from me now . . . as far as the well-fed French people who once plucked the shells with me from their willow baskets on the rue de la Gare, when the old man sliced open the rough long shells with his knife there or in front of Crespin's in Dijon in the winter, and the little oyster-stalls stood bravely near the stations in all the province-towns of France. The greenness and the tepid brassiness of those shellfish were at first a shock, and I also thought I should suspect their unhygienic deaths . . . but none ever hurt me, and my palate always benefited as well as my spirit.

In America I think I like best the oysters from Long Island Sound, although I have eaten Chincoteagues and some others from the Delaware Bay that were very good. Farther south, in spite of my innate enthusiasm, I have had to admit that the oysters grow less interesting served in the shell, and almost cry out for such delicious decadences as horseradish or even cooking, which would be sacrilege in Boston or Bordeaux.

On the Mexican Gulf they are definitely better cooked, although skilled gourmets have insisted otherwise to me, and one man from Corpus Christi once put his gun on the table while he stated quietly that anybody who said Texas blue points weren't the best anywhere was more than one kind of insulting liar. I still prefer cooked oysters in the South, since for me one of the pleasures of eating a raw oyster is the crispness of its flesh (*crisp* is not quite right, and *flesh* is not right, but in the same way you might say that *oyster* is not right for what I mean) . . . and crispness seems not to exist in the warm waters there.

And on the West Coast, I like the metallic tiny bites of the Olympias, and patriotism or no patriotism, find the Japanese-spawned Willapoints from Oregon tasteless and too bulky to be eaten from the shell. One thing, to my mind, should accompany all such oysters served this way as inevitably as soda crackers go with soup in a drugstore or Gilbert with Sullivan or Happy New Year with Merry Christmas: buttered brown bread and lemon.

In the Good Old Days, those good old days so dull to hear about and so delightful to talk of, thin slices of real pumpernickel-ish brown bread (No machine-sliced beige-colored sponge, for God's sake!) and honest-to-Betsy lumps of juicy lemon used to come automatically with every half-dozen of oysters, whether you sat in the circle at the Café de Paris or stood with one foot in the sawdust down near the third-class restaurant of the Nurnberger-Bahnhof. They picked up the sometimes tired flavor of the oysters, and I soon discovered that a few drops of lemon juice on the buttered bread tasted much better than on the shellfish themselves.

I have thought seriously about this, while incendiary bombs fell and people I knew were maimed and hungry, and I believe that all American oyster-bars and every self-respecting restaurant in this good land that presumes to serve raw oysters in their shells or even naked in a cup, should at once make it compulsory to serve also a little plate of thin-sliced nicely buttered good dark bread, preferably the heavy fine-grained kind and buttered with sweet butter I should say, and a few quarters of lemon.

I think the oyster-men and the owners of restaurants would find this little persnicket a paying one, and that even if they charged a few cents extra for the lemon or the butter or even the bread, like Lipp's and some of the old places in Europe, they would sell enough more oysters to repay them many times.

And for the person who likes oysters, such a delicate, charming, nostalgic gesture would seem so delicate, so nostalgically charming, so reminiscent of a thousand good mouthfuls here and there in the past . . . in other words, so *sensible* . . . that it would make even nostalgia less a perversion than a lusty bit of nourishment.

Pearls Are
Not Good to Eat

Pearls are calcareous concretions of peculiar lustre, produced
by certain molluscs, and valued as objects of personal
adornment.

Encyclopædia Britannica

There are several things to do with oysters beside eat them, although many people believe firmly in that as the most sensible
course.

Oysters themselves (that is, the living creatures within their
shells) can harbor little crabs called, plainly enough, oyster-
crabs. They are about the size of a six-year-old girl's thumb-
nail, and look exactly like a normal crab seen through the wrong
end of an opera glass, square and ruddy and well fringed with
legs and such. They are one of the most delicious delicate by-
products in the world, on land or sea.

It is perhaps only a gastronomical coincidence that they seem
to be the most numerous when whitebait are in season, but the
combination so often met with in New York and other Eastern
cities about Christmastime is perfect: tiny crisp fried oyster-
crabs and little almost formless fish about an inch long, piled on

plates big enough for humans but still looking like something prepared for a banquet at the court of Lilliput. They are served with lemon and parsley, either fresh or fried, and watercress is good with them too. So is champagne. So, really, is beer, light and cold.

There may be other things than crabs about the oysters themselves that can be used by humans, but I do not know them. Of course there are various catsups and spices that are made, all over the world but especially in China, but they cannot properly be called other than food. And once the oyster is dismissed and the shell is considered, gastronomy takes second place.

Oyster shell will probably never be called good to eat, unless by certain worms and by hens, who are, perhaps fortunately, mute on the subject of *la gourmandise*. They have been nibbling on shells for centuries without too much protest, and the more eggs they lay the more they love to peck into their little boxes of nice sharp oyster shell. Calcium and lime are to them, apparently, as instinctive a necessity as the fine dreams to a confirmed opium smoker, so that in spite of themselves they must have the wherewithal. In the case of the hens the problem is a simple one, and farmers and their wives in no-matter-what far country can buy crushed shell for their barnyards.

It is only near the seacoasts, though, that oyster shells are used for roads and ditch-linings and such rougher businesses, and there certainly you would not find a gastronomic connection . . . unless for remembering, with farfetched romanticism, that every shell once held its tasty lodger, which must have been swallowed somewhere, by someone, before the road could be paved.

In Louisiana, in the winter between rains, the edges of the high causeways over the bayous and paddies are white and sharp-looking with tons of pounded shells. They hold back the mud like mortar, and past them the flat dead rice fields look soft and treacherous. If the wheel of your car slips off the road there is a high squealing crunch, and all the birds eating rice grains near the flocks of little cows fly up for a second, and then settle again around the ruminating beasts.

The best known of all an oyster's parasites (if anything as crisp and delicate and tiny as a crab could be called such) and all its by-products of chicken-scratch and paving-crumbs and even catsups, is something that for centuries has meant love and bloody battle to mankind: the pearl.

In India and China and even in the chill courts of Scottish kings, pearls have been set in metal and hung from pins and chains as long as such things existed. And they have never been thought cheap.

They grow slowly, secretly, gleaming "worm-coffins" built in what may be pain around the bodies that have crept inside the shells. Sometimes it is indeed a kind of tapeworm, a larva that bores deep into the oyster's soft flesh, carrying as it goes some particles of the creature's injured mantle. These particles take with them their power to start the secretion of the same mother-of-pearl that lines the shell, rather as yeast carried from one sourdough pot to another fresh one will start its business all over again. And ultimately the unwelcome worm is encased in its rare coffin, and within the two shells lies a pearl.

(Some quibblers think, and who can say how well or wrongly, that water-mites on ducks cause pearls, and the *Encyclopædia Britannica* says that "many different exciting causes" may lead to their formation. But, worms or lice or other excitations, pearls still enchant mankind.)

They can be flat on one side, never quite free within the shell, and then they are called "*boutons*." They can be hollow, warty blisters, "*coq de perle*," or they can be irregular and "*baroque*." They are all valuable. To be of the first water, though, they must be perfectly spherical, or symmetrically pear-shaped, like a tear without its imagined point, and skin and orient must satisfy: that is, their texture must be delicate and flawless, of an almost translucent white, and their sheen must be subdued and yet iridescent. It is surprising, really, that there are so many correct ones in the world: pink, quickly fading, from the West Indies; the rare black ones from Mexico; white ones everywhere.

As far as can be known, pearls grow best in stunted, irregular shells, and almost everywhere in the world where there is at least a short period of warmth, since it is then that the secretion takes place every year. Any time after their fourth year they are worth finding.

In India and the southern seas, where most pearls are found, the divers bring up perhaps a thousand shells for every one with a jewel in it, and consider the hunting good. In rivers, from Japan to Ireland to our own state of Iowa, such ratios are unknown, and only the fact that pearls are actually there, somewhere, makes the fishers keep on their tedious work.

The job is not an easy one, and pearl-divers are short-lived. Soemtimes their lungs burst. Sometimes they are killed by sharks, who live almost always near the oysterbeds, so that the divers must go armed with knives or ironwood spikes. Things have not changed much anywhere since Marco Polo wrote of the pearl grounds off the Malabar, on the south shores of Coromandel.

In the fisheries, he says, the merchants always arranged for "certain enchanters belonging to a class of Brahmans" to sit in the boats accompanying the divers, and to utter spells, so that the numerous fierce sharks that roamed the waters thereabouts should not attack. And at night these wizards discontinued their spells and magical cantations so that the sharks might patrol the places and thus in their own way act as police against other robbers.

Marco Polo could see the same enchanters in the pearl boats

off India now, and probably hear the same spells, for sharks still live hardly less dangerously than the divers they attack, and pearls are still worth men's lives.

In Japan and China it is girls who do the diving, but they risk little, for the pearls they seek are not forty feet deep and uncharted, but only a few feet down and put there cannily by men who have been growing such rare jewels like sea-radishes for hundreds of years.

The girls wear queer rumpled turbans, and flop into the water at regular intervals, several at a time, like drunken birds. Ninety percent of their shells have pearls in them, and if from disease and general bad luck only five percent of the whole fishing is marketable, the merchants feel fat and happy. For cultured pearls are so beautiful that they can only be told from "natural" ones by X ray, and in spite of their elaborate care, they are still a profitable crop.

In China, until recently at least, there had been an ancient market in Soochow where pearls in the shape of the Buddha could be bought, or even tiny fish or rings or lewder symbols. They were made carefully by men who put the matrices carefully into the shells in May or June: images of wood or tin or lead. Then the oysters were fattened for three years or so in tubs of seawater well spiked with human dung, and when the time was ripe the beautiful images were sold to the religious and the curious, and the oysters were enjoyed in the kitchen. (Probably, since the Chinese are a thorough race, the shells were used in building walls, and thus full value received from the unprotesting bivalve.)

Pearls have been cultivated all over the world, even in Sweden, but probably the Japanese have been most persistently successful, so that the following recipe must be carried out somewhere in the coastal waters of Nippon, just as most such rules should be followed in kitchens or pantries.

To Make a Pearl

1 *healthy spat*	*scrubbing brushes, etc.*
1 *mature oyster*	*unnameable wound-*
1 *bead*	*astringent provided by*
1 *wire cage*	*Japanese government*
ligatures	1 *diving-girl*

Introduce the spat, which should be at least ⅟₇₅ of an inch long, to the smooth surface of the cage. Submerge him in quiet clean water, where the cage will protect him from starfish, and frequent inspections and scrubbings will keep his rapidly growing shell free from boring-worms and such pests.

In three years prepare him for the major operation of putting the bead on his mantle (epithelium). Once the bead is in place, draw the mantle over it and ligature the tissues to form a wee sac. Put the sac into the second oyster, remove the ligature, treat the wound with the unnameable astringent, and after the oyster has been caged, put him into the sea.

Supervise things closely for seven years, with the help of your diving-girl. Any time after that you may open your oyster, and you have about one chance in twenty of owning a marketable pearl, and a small but equally exciting chance of having cooked up something really valuable.

It may be felt by some people that a simpler process would be to eat oysters until a pearl appeared. That is even longer, however, and in many years of oyster-eating and oyster-talking, the only person I have ever met who found one is myself.

It was at Galatoire's, in New Orleans, and for a few seconds after I almost cracked my tooth on the jewel, I sat in a reeling dream of riches and royalties, while the fine noisy odorous room grew dim around me. All the tweedy debutantes with their dark hair lying on their shoulders, and the thin Jews eating *pompano en papillotte* quietly while their friends drank, and the military men in civilian clothes and the high-class courtesans in uniform, and the politicians and reporters watching everyone in the mirrors between delicious mouthfuls: all that danced about me in an odor of fish and wine and general gastronomic sanctity. My head was filled with phrases: pearl of great price, pearls before swine, of Orient pearl a double row, Cleopatra's "pearl dissolved in royal wine," pearls on snow. . . .

Finally I worked my excitement into audible form and the pearl toward the front of my mouth, but by the time everyone around me knew what had happened and I had spat it fairly genteelly into my hand, I knew without looking at it what I would see.

It was a small, brownish, rough thing, rather like an abnormally dingy piece of gravel, and I put it by my plate to take home, and forgot it when I finally left the restaurant. It *was* exciting for a few minutes, even though I agreed thoroughly with the Chinese proverb that "Pearls and Precious Stones are not good to eat or drink."

Those Were Happy Days

An old gentleman t'other day in discourse with a friend of his
(reflecting upon some adventures they had in youth
together), cry'd out, Oh Jack, those were happy days!

The Spectator, RICHARD STEELE

There are stories that in their telling spread about them a feeling
of the Golden Age, so that when you listen you forget all but the
warmth and incredible excitement of those other farther times;
oysters can be as fine as Ozymandias king of kings in them, and
as unforgettable.

I shall remember always the mysterious beautiful sensation
of well-being I felt, when I was small, to hear my mother talk of
the suppers she used to eat at boarding school. They were called
"midnight feasts," and were kept secret, supposedly, from the
teachers, in the best tradition of the 1890s. They consisted of
oyster loaf. There may have been other things. Maybe the most
daring young ladies even drank ginger beer, although I am
afraid it was more likely a sweet raspberry shrub or some such
unfortunate potation. Maybe there were cigarettes, and pick-
les, and bonbons. But it is the oyster loaf that I remember.

I know I shall never taste one like it, except in my dreams, nor
will my mother . . . if she ever really did so. But I can see it, and

smell it, and I even know which parts to bite and which to let melt against the roof of my mouth, exquisitely hot and comforting, although my mother surely never told me.

It was made in a bread loaf from the best baker in the village, and the loaf was hollowed out and filled with rich cooked oysters, and then, according to my mother's vague and yet vivid account, the top of the loaf was fastened on again, and the whole was baked crisp and brown in the oven. Then it was wrapped tightly in a fine white napkin, and hidden under a chambermaid's cape while she ran from the baker's to the seminary and up the back stairs to the appointed bedroom.

The girls, six or seven of them because an oyster loaf was really very large, sat in their best flowered wrappers on the floor, while one of them kept watch at the keyhole and saw that no light flickered from her candle or the shaded lamp.

The maid slipped into the whispering, giggling huddle, and put down her warm bundle, and although she had been well paid was always willing to take a pocketful of the rich cookies the young ladies' mothers sent them every week from home. Then she left, and the oyster loaf was unwrapped.

Now, today, it may sound untidy and foolish and a fine prelude to biliousness, but then there was something exciting and good about such schoolgirl *gourmandise*, so that when my mother told me of it, I thought with the old gentleman in *The Spectator* that those were indeed happy days, happier than I could ever know myself.

After I grew up I always looked under *oysters* in any cookbooks I happened to be using, to see what was said about oyster loaves. It was not that I planned to make one: I simply remembered, once again, my mother's casual reminiscence. Usually the recipe was more or less like this one, from André Simon's *French Cook Book*:[1]

[1]Little, Brown and Company, Boston, 1938.

Pain d'huitres
(Oyster Loaf)

Put into a bowl 2½ ounces of finely sifted bread crumbs, work into them 2 ounces of butter, season with seasoning salt; add 3 yolks, the liquid obtained from 2 dozen sauce oysters, and the oysters themselves, bearded and cut into dice.

Line a well-buttered charlotte mold with fish forcemeat about an inch thick; put the oyster mixture into the hollow, cover it with more of the forcemeat, and poach very gently for about 45 minutes.

Of course this is an exceedingly tony version, which Monsieur Simon admits he got from an Englishman, of what can be a pretty crude and terrible kind of stodgy meat loaf made of inferior oysters, which is sold sometimes in bad restaurants along the Atlantic Coast. I have seen it, but have fortunately been talked out of tasting it, even for research purposes. Monsieur Simon's recipe is a good one . . . but still it has no connection with the one my mother talked of.

I have found one or two that were more or less as they ought to be, but still my mind's palate, educated to the smooth hot perfection of that "midnight feast," has known that they were poor things really. Even Mrs. Simon Kander, who usually tempers the cold practicability of her *Settlement Cook Book*[2] with her innate Jewish warmth, disappointed me with a dull recipe for "Oysters in Crust Cases."

Finally, a few years ago, I found in the *Sunset's All-Western Cook Book*[3] a whole column called, praise be, "Oyster Loaf." It gave three or four ways to make what it implied, with pardonable insularity, was a dish particularly appreciated by San Franciscans, and at least one of its rules sounded, at long last, much as I have always hoped my mother's schoolgirl feast should be.

[2]Milwaukee, 1931.
[3]Genevieve A. Callahan, Lane Publishing Company, San Francisco, 1935.

Sunset recommends, among other things, filling a hollowed-out loaf with an oyster-and-bread stuffing such as you put in a turkey, and then baking it, slicing it, and serving it with a cream or cheese sauce.

It says you can fill hollowed-out French or finger rolls with creamed oysters, which you then bake and serve very hot.

It gives some more recipes.

But the one that makes me like the whole thing with an almost affectionate nostalgic liking is this:

Oyster Loaf

Cut off the top of a crusty loaf of bread, and hollow out the center. Brush with butter, and put into a hot oven to heat through and toast slightly. While this is going on, coat medium-sized oysters with egg and crumbs, and fry them brown in deep or shallow fat. Fill the loaf with the oysters, pour melted butter over them, put on the lid which also has been toasted, and it is ready to eat . . . or to wrap thickly in wax paper and take on a picnic. A small loaf to serve two people is most convenient for serving.

For me at least, that recipe is at last the one I have been looking for. I can change it as I will, and even pour a little thick cream over the loaf, or dust it with cayenne, but basically it is right with my childhood dream . . . and quite probably it is much better than the one the young ladies ate in their stuffy lamp-lit rendezvous so many years ago.

And yet . . . yet those will always be, in my mental gastronomy, on my spiritual taste-buds, the most delicious oysters I never ate.

Oh, Mother, those were happy days!

Soup of the Evening,
Beautiful Soup

All ought to be made to taste the soup . . .
Grimm's Fairy Tales

This is not that, and that certainly is not this, and at the same time an oyster stew is not stewed, and although they are made of the same things and even cooked almost the same way, an oyster soup should never be called a stew, nor a stew soup. It is perfectly clear, if you respect oysters and the words about them, and are annoyed by home economics articles, complete with soup recipes, which begin, "Dress up your oyster stew . . ."

An oyster stew is made quickly, about as fast as the hand can follow the mind or the mind the eye. Oyster soup takes longer, can cost much or little, and pleases some people even more than it bores others.

The great difference between it and the stew, probably, is that the soup has a thickening in it of flour or crumbs or egg, or, as one precise chef says, "*Rice! Never* flour or cornstarch!" It is richer, and yet oddly enough is often served before a large meal, whereas oyster stew is considered by even the heaviest gourmands as a meal in itself.

An inexpensive soup that tastes more like oysters than its recipe would lead you to suspect, especially if you have been reading older rules that call nonchalantly for quarts and pails, is the following, found in a newspaper:

Cream of Oyster Soup

¼ *cup butter*	1 *teaspoon salt*
2 *tablespoons flour*	¼ *teaspoon celery salt*
1 *quart milk*	*dash pepper*
½ *pint oysters(!)*	

Melt butter in top of double boiler, remove from heat, and blend in flour. Add milk and stir constantly over direct heat until mixture boils and thickens slightly. Add seasonings and place over boiling water; cover. Remove any bits of shell from oysters. Chop oysters, using chopping bowl; add with liquor to hot mixture, heat thoroughly, approximately ten minutes, and serve piping hot with crisp crackers or buttered toast rings and strips. Serves six.

This recipe, especially when boxed on a newspaper page with its accompanying photograph, smudged but still modern in the Let-Us-Keep-Our-Kitchens-Gay manner, is almost actively abhorrent. It represents, with its efficiency, its lack of imagination, its very practicability, everything that Brillat-Savarin, in his forthright manner, would have belched at gastronomically.

And yet it can be a good soup. Basically it is well constructed, and, most valuable, it allows for certain extremely personal deviations: a pinch of fresh marjoram buds by Mrs. Zanzibar Woodbury, herbologist extraordinary of the East Dingle-Dell Garden Club; a dash of dry sherry by Y. Erpington Grubb, *bon-vivant*-emeritus of the English department of Stokes-on-the-Hudson College for Young Gentlemen; a rousing grind of fresh pepper by Charles (Chub) Bye, late of the Left Bank and later still of assorted Southern and Far Western "artists' colonies." The lady and the professor and the chubby yearner have reason; any addition, or all, to this sterile recipe can do small harm, and at best make it yet plainer that basically it is good enough to stand well-nigh incredible assaults, even to using tinned oysters.

Other rules for soup are less amenable. One that sounds almost like the newspaper recipe, and comes from the *New England Cook Book*, could no more be made with Number 2 cans of steamed Willapoints than Flying Fortresses with matchboxes . . . and as for imaginative additions, a flick of paprika is probably as far as even the most sacrilegious gourmet should let himself go:

Oyster Soup

1 *quart oysters*	2 *tablespoons flour*
3 *cups milk*	1½ *teaspoon salt*
1 *cup cream*	¼ *teaspoon pepper*
3 *tablespoons butter*	1 *tablespoon grated onion*

Melt the butter and stir in the flour and blend well. Slowly add the milk, stirring all the time, then the cream and seasonings, and grated onion. Keep hot over a low flame. Bring the oysters to a boil in their own liquor. Cook about 5 minutes or until the edges curl. Strain. Add oysters to the milk stock, heat about 5 minutes without boiling. Serve immediately.

Some books, less blunt in their manner than the austere New England pamphlet, call their soups bisques, and in general such a change of wording indicates either richer ingredients or a more finicky rule of procedure, with perhaps a few words of kitchen French thrown casually in with the English. Equally in general, such recipes are excellent.

One of them, given in Merle Armitage's *Fit for a King*, is a good model for all such rules:

Oyster Bisque

Make a roux of butter and flour. Add a large onion finely chopped and brown the mixture. Then add a quart of boiling water, 4 dozen oysters and their liquor, a generous square of butter, bay leaf, thyme, and salt and pepper. Boil this soup for 20 minutes, then remove 2 dozen of the oysters and chop them finely. Then pass the soup and the rest of the oysters through a sieve, mashing the oysters. Now add the chopped oysters and 4 sprigs of parsley. Serve steaming.

Mrs. William Vaughan Moody, who can always be trusted to cope with any of the finer problems of American gastronomy, also calls her soup bisque, and adds, as is her wont, a good gout of whipped cream, which almost, but not quite, makes her recipe "ladies' luncheon":

Oyster Bisque[1]

---

1 quart of oysters	½ cup of cracker crumbs
1 pint of cream	onion
1 pint of milk	salt, pepper, paprika
1 cup of whipped cream	mace

Put the oysters over to heat in a dish by themselves.

Put the pint of milk and the pint of cream in a double boiler, with a sprig of mace, and half a sweet onion. Remove the onion and mace when their first flavor is imparted.

When the oysters, and the milk and cream are hot, strain out the oys-

---

[1]Mrs. William Vaughan Moody's Cook Book.

ters, and put the liquor into the hot milk. Throw the oysters into cold water. Skim off any froth that rises to the top of the mixture in the double boiler. Add pepper and salt to taste, ½ cup of cracker crumbs, and 1 tablespoon of sweet butter. Let all cook together for a few minutes until the soup is well blended.

Strain the water off the oysters. Dry them on a clean piece of cheesecloth. Put them into the soup and serve at once, with a tablespoon of whipped cream on each cup.

Mrs. Moody's literary style, or rather aroma, is almost as delicate as her genteel methods for making a soup taste like onion without having any onion showing in the final dish, and there are some irreverent souls who will follow her excellent rule even to putting the bisque in the cups and the whipped cream on the bisque, and then destroy her delicacy with a hearty tap of cayenne pepper over each rich melting mound. Such behavior is audacious, but in spite of evidence to the contrary, it is hard to believe that Mrs. Moody herself would not approve of it.

The recipe (or, as she called it, the receipt) set forth by Marion Harland in her *Common Sense in the Household* is, surprisingly enough, the most elaborate. Of course, in the 1870s in eastern America there was a plenitude of what that good woman winningly called "girls," along with most other housewives of our land, and even "second girls" were common in houses that today boast nothing more efficient than a vacuum cleaner and an electric dishwasher. Mrs. Harland, although much more sensible than most of her colleagues, still gauged recipes and their construction in terms of hours spent by Irish scullery maids rather than minutes dashed off by wives just home from the office. For that reason, as well as others, her rules are as quaint as Elizabethan diaries by now, and yet are practical, if carried out with a grain or two of that common sense she so heartily recommends:

Oyster Soup (Number 2)

2 quarts of oysters	1 qt. milk
2 eggs	1 teacupful of water

Strain the liquor from the oysters into a saucepan, pour in with it the water. Season with cayenne pepper and a little salt, a teaspoonful of mingled nutmeg, mace, and cloves. When the liquor is almost boiling, add half the oysters chopped finely and boil 5 minutes quite briskly. Strain the soup and return to saucepan with the milk. Have ready some forcemeat balls, not larger than marbles, made of the yolks of the eggs boiled hard and rubbed to a smooth paste with a little butter, then mixed with 6 raw oysters chopped very finely, a little salt, and a raw egg well beaten, to bind the ingredients together. Flour your hands well and roll the forcemeat into pellets, laying them upon a cold plate, so as not to touch one another, until needed. Then put the reserved whole oysters into the hot soup, and when it begins to boil again, drop in the forcemeat marbles. Boil until the oysters "ruffle," by which time the balls will also be done.

Serve with sliced lemon and crackers. A liberal tablespoonful of butter stirred in gently at the last is an improvement.

Everyone, from Mrs. Harland to the anonymous ascetic New Englanders and back again to various extollers of the elegant bisque, agrees that Oyster Soup is something made with cream and thickening . . . and oysters, whole or chopped, fresh (God willing) or even tinned.

But there is a way to make a soup from oysters that demands only oysters. Oysters there *must* be, and for the rest, you make or even pour from a tin the best beef consommé you can get, and heat it and put in the cold washed shellfish. Then you put an unbroken egg yolk tenderly into each soup-plate, and pour the consommé with its multitude of oysters over it, in a gentle way so that the yolk will cook a little and stay whole. That is all. It is quick, and easy, and it is good, too.

Love Was the Pearl

Then love was the pearl of his oyster,
And Venus rose red out of wine.
                    Dolores, C. A. SWINBURNE

The love-life of an oyster is a curious one, dependent on the vagaries of temperature and the tides. If its world is warm, if the water around it is about seventy degrees, it is able to send out a little potent flood of milt and thus excite a female to her monstrous spawning, now five million eggs, now fifty. And if the tide is right, the milt will meet the eggs, and spats will result.

Spatting and spawning, spawning and spatting . . .

The love-life of a man has also been called curious, and part of it has long depended on the mysterious powers of this bivalved mollusc that most of the dictionaries say is usually eaten alive.

Women have been known to be influenced, and whether to the good or nay is not for me to say, by the schemed use of these shellfish, and there is one man named Mussolini who lives near Biloxi, in Mississippi, who swears that he has cured seven frigid virgins by the judicious feeding of long brownish buck-oysters from nearby bayous.

It is men, though, in astounding numbers, who will swear,

in correctly modulated voices, a hundred equally strange facts. Women of the East, they will tell you if you are acceptable for such confessions, are built crossways, so that lovemaking is even more exotic than erotic with them. They know it for a fact. And there is an equally astounding number of men, and some of them have actually graduated from Yale, and even Princeton, who know positively that oysters are an aphrodisiac . . . one of the best. They can tell of countless chaps whose powers have been increased nigh unto the billy goat's, simply from eating raw cold oysters.

There are many reasons why an oyster is supposed to have this desirable quality, embarrassing if true . . . and although the term is literally incorrect, most of them are old wives' tales.

Most of them are physiological, too, and have to do with an oyster's odor, its consistency, and probably its strangeness. All of them, apparently, are fond but false hopes, and no more to be relied on than that a horsehair dropped into a trough in the full of the moon will swim about and hiss, an honest-to-God snake.

There was a thin little man once, at Harvard probably. He was not quite a virgin, being about twenty-two years old, and for some reason he managed to date himself, one wintry Saturday night, with a very very terrible very very divine girl of the upper classes known by young men of the same classes as La Belle Dame sans Culottes.

The thin little man, hardly more than a lad as his Grandfather used to say, felt full of tremblings and awed withdrawals, and consulted with several of his more obviously virile friends. Oysters, they said firmly. Oysters are the answer.

So about noon on the dated Saturday the chapkin dropped in at the Grand Central Oyster Bar. It was December, and the oysters, raw and chilled, were not only delicious but correctly in season for any and all correct young men. Ours bolstered himself with some ale, all by himself but still thinking of it (since

English B4 with good old pipe-smoking Cyril Dinwiddie) as a noggin rather than a glass, and ate one dozen more than he really wanted.

About two o'clock he was horrified to see that it was not three, and roamed thinly into the cold streets, his mind trying with a dawning hopelessness to call up some of the more torrid reminiscences of his approaching date . . . reminiscences of his roommates, that is.

He took a taxi to the Plaza Grill, looked with what jauntiness he could summon at the raddled brokers eating delicious things like scrambled eggs and hot baked potatoes, and ordered another dozen oysters. He wished it was about six o'clock . . . by then there would at least be one or two lovely actresses to peek at, and he would be within an hour of . . . of . . .

He ordered another dozen.

A little later he walked over to Sixth Avenue and headed boggily toward the RKO Gateway. He had always liked oyster-bars. He had always thought they were fun, removed as they were for the most part from the shrill chitterings of debutantes. But now, as it grew dark and people scuttled for busses all about him, he began to think that a sweet little debutante sipping her tea-and-martinis at "21" would be heaven. He could pay the bill when she was finished with her childlike pleasures, take her to her mother's safely respectable elevator . . . and go home.

But tonight he was meeting the Belle of the Balls . . . and alone . . .

He turned into the Gateway, and in a small hopeless voice ordered two dozen blue points.

When the barman peered at him he snapped, in a masculine way he hoped, "That's what I said, isn't it?" For a minute he felt almost warmed by his own unsuspected fire, and then as he started diligently to swallow his prescription he was nearly overcome by a dreadful weariness, so that if he had not represented the Alma Mater he surmised he did, he would have stretched out quietly on the soft-looking white tile floor and given himself to safe dreams.

Instead, he pulled in his stomach as far as he could, and sipped seemingly at his ale, and gradually ate two dozen more of the same.

About six-thirty at night, this thin little man, looking much older than twenty-two for the first time in his life, walked slowly and uncertainly up the steps of the Harvard or whatever Club. Visions of rosy flesh and honey-colored thighs were quite wiped out, at last, by the chill certainty that Old Chick and Old Bill and Old Rot-Gut had betrayed him. Yes, he was betrayed . . . thank God.

Bed, he thought solemnly. Bed is what I need . . . and *alone*. I'm still a man, he thought with his last remaining spark of masculinity . . . I'm still a man, in *spite* of the blasted shellfish . . .

And he stuck out his chest and almost fell flat on his peaked oyster-colored face.

"Here, *here*, sir," the porter clucked, feeling somewhat wearily that another chance to prove himself a real father stared him in the face. "Not *here*, sir. You just come with me."

And he tucked his arm winningly, seductively, with practiced skill, into the thin little man's, and together they wove toward a comfortable couch.

My Country, 'Tis of Thee

The oyster cocktail is a cocktail, no? As is the Martini? Then they are together on the menu . . . and besides, it is already printed. Why change it?

MEXICAN MAITRE D'HOTEL

International confusion in restaurants can be terrible or it can be utterly-mad-and-amusing, depending entirely upon the gastronomic humor of the diners. I have seen three Englishmen eating Algerian couscous and drinking great swigs of a particularly rich Tokay Aszu in a little Spanish café in Switzerland, and because of their goodwill enjoying it, in spite of its basically horrible mélange of flavors, as much as the refugees around them who ate hare cooked in olive oil from their own town of Madrid and squirted thin *vino rojo* into their faces from the common long-nosed carafe.

Usually it is most fortunate, if you are eating something Russian, to drink what a Russian would like to drink with it . . . or its nearest equivalent. Vodka is fine with caviar, but if you have no vodka (and do have the other, which seems highly improbable these days) a glass of dry gin is far from heretical.

In the same way a pint of old-and-mild goes with a cut off the joint at Simpson's, but if you are safely distant from staunch London's Strand and its present preoccupation with things other than the pleasures of the table, you can do yourself passably well with a glass of good local beer and a slice of roast beef, even in a Connecticut hamburger-joint or a fabulous California "drive-in."

Oysters, being almost universal, can be and have been eaten with perhaps a wider variety of beverages than almost any other dish I can think of . . . and less disastrously. They lend themselves to the whims of every cool and temperate climate, so that one man can drink wine with them, another beer, and another fermented buttermilk, and no man will be wrong.

Patriotism is always present, of course, so that it is almost as difficult for a Frenchman to watch you drink anything but wine with your slate-blue, black-gilled Portugaises as it is for him to imagine cooking them. There is a strong feeling in almost every Gallic heart that heating an oyster makes it infamous, such that even such a reputable gourmet as Paul Reboux must preface any recipe for cooking them with cajolery. "I understand," he says at the beginning of "Baked Oysters" in his *Plats du Jour*, "that you haven't much sympathy for hot oysters. But . . . perhaps you could bring yourself to try the recipe that follows?"

The Portugaise and the rarer European (*Ostrea edulis*) should be eaten in one way, and one only, a Frenchman thinks . . . and therefore he feels with some firmness that all other oysters in the world should be so treated. It should be opened at street temperature in a cool month, never iced, and plucked from its rough irregular shell at once, so that its black gills still vibrate and cringe with the shock of the air upon them. It should be swallowed, not too fast, and then its fine salt juices, more like the smell of rock pools at low tide than any other food in the world, should be drunk at one gulp from the shell. Then, of course, a bite or two of buttered brown bread must follow, better to stimulate the *papilles* . . . and then, of course, of course, a fine mouthful of a white wine.

The safest wine, probably, to order with these winter pleasures is a good Chablis. It travels well, and if it is poured at the same temperature as the oysters it can be good whether it comes in a bottle from the Valmur vineyard's best vintage or in a carafe with the questionable name "Chablis Village."

On the other hand, I have had Pouilly-Fuissé, various kinds of champagnes *nature*, a pink Peau d'Onion, and both bottled and open wines of Anjou with oysters in France, and whether they were correctly drunk or not, I was. Nobody knew it except my own exhilarated senses and my pleased mind, all of which must enter into any true gastronomic experience.

In England ales are the rule with the fat round oysters of the coastal beds, and any pub can recommend its own brew when the season's on. And of course sherry is safe.

It is partly because wines are dear that Britishers stick so firmly to their ales, but a small amount of good stiff patriotism, I suspect, makes most of them insist that anything else kills the flavor of their famous shellfish. Myself, I have drunk good and fairly inexpensive *steinwein* from Wurzburg in a small restaurant in Liverpool, and had other people enjoying their own oysters with a glass of Guinness whisper about me as I ate mine. Needless to say, I have also drunk Guinness with the best of them, and thought, at least temporarily, that the British were right—about their oysters anyway.

Here at home we can, and do, drink what we want, and not always with such fortunate results as the more custom-bound Europeans get from their rigid rules and recipes. In London, once, I knew a Yankee who threw a small pub into shocked worried silence by drinking three whiskeys and then eating a plate of cold raw Whitestaples. Everyone watched him as if at any moment he might fall into a fit or turn bottle-green, and when he left, the barmaid asked a constable to see him to his hotel, convinced as she was that that hard liquor would turn the oysters in him to some poisonous kind of rubber.

Unfortunately that is almost true, and it is foolish thus to cook the poor fish before they can say scat or realize that they've been swallowed. Another reason, perhaps even more important esthetically, is that anything as strong as whiskey or gin or brandy will sear, in a way, the delicate surface of a human's palate, so that if he drinks before he swallows his oysters, the theory is that he might as well eat soft tar or egg-white for all the pleasure his taste buds can give him.

It is still the custom here, though, to have a cocktail or so before a meal, or in an oyster-bar to have a couple of quickies while the shells are being opened. We continue to drink, and we continue to eat millions of oysters every year . . . and we continue, perversely, to enjoy them probably as much as the Frenchman with his white wine and the Britisher with his ale.

We can, and often do, drink good white wine from California, or light beers, because we are perhaps the least insular gourmands of any in the world. But most often we do what we like best, regardless of custom, and pour ourselves a good stiff drink as prelude to that most sensitive of foods, the oyster. And live to tell it.

As Luscious as Locusts

The best in this kind are but shadows . . .
A Midsummer Night's Dream,
WILLIAM SHAKESPEARE

There is a little book called *Eloge de la Gourmandise,* one of those thin witty pompous books that have appeared for decades in the Paris bookshops, in which Jean-Louis Vaudoyer speaks of a woman he once watched eat something especially delicious.

She savored her enjoyment with a carefully sensual slowness, and then she sighed, as it came to its inevitable end, "Ah . . . what a pity that I do not have little taste-buds clear to the bottom of my stomach!"

Such a remark could not seem anything but gross to an ascetic man, partly because a woman said it and partly because all such frank gastronomic pleasures are inexplicable to him. The joys of the table are not within his ken, and therefore he suspects, with some possible rightness, their devotees.

And yet to a man who has once eaten something and taken thought about it . . . not merely digested it and remembered that, but eaten, digested, and then *thought* . . . such a blatantly sensual remark as that made by Vaudoyer's friend is not only comprehensible but highly intelligent.

Almost every man keeps in his own mind a few such intense

moments, when his senses combine with his vocabulary to make him say some such spontaneous and even shocking thing about a taste or a whole dish. And after, when he remembers, he thinks, "That was the best melon, or pheasant, or sausage, I ever ate in my life." He means it.

Often the place and the time help make a certain food what it becomes, even more than the food itself. Vaudoyer does not say when, or why, his companion made her epic comment on *la gourmandise*, but it is easy to imagine her a beautiful, gently rounded woman with dark eyes and dainty wrists, who ate with delicate avidity at a ripe peach after a summer afternoon full of love. It is easy, and pleasant too . . .

In the same way you can remember hearing an old fisherman in a little bar in southern Delaware say to the room with real solemnity, "Them was the best God-damned swimpses I ever et," and you wonder about him and his life and his shrimp-nets and what the day was like when he ate his own catch.

There is a man in California who used to know George Sterling and Jack London and such foggy minor gods, and who now, inevitably, has become to the young coastal yearners almost as mythical as his dead friends. He holds what might be called soirées, and malicious critics suspect, not too silently, that his famous booming laugh and his broad quips at these parties, which a few years ago would still be called Bohemian, contain almost as much corn as they do bourbon. Nevertheless he is no worse than any valiant shadow, and when he is alone, free for a few minutes from the midgelike clouds of admiring college people who usually surround him, his voice grows quiet and his face sags and he talks to himself out loud of other days.

"Hang Town Fry," he'll say, tenderly and practically at the drop of a hat. "Hang Town Fry!"

Then, when he doesn't say any more, you realize that he is at last serious, if not sober, and you ask him, "What about it?"

"What about Hang Town Fry? You don't know? And you

call yourself a San Franciscan? Why, it's the best food that ever sat before misbegotten man, and early in the morning with a hard day ahead, or before that when you're wondering why you did it, or at night for a nice supper with your girl . . . Why, Hang Town Fry . . . I remember once . . ."

Then, for a few minutes or seconds before the part he has been playing so long submerges his real thinking self, and smudges all the outlines into those of a campus character, you see what this big deaf lost man must have been, one night down near the Ferry Building when he ate Hang . . . Town . . . Fry. . . .

This is the way it was made, if his beer-joint had a decent Chinese cook as they all did in those times. Why it was the best thing in the world to him you can never know, but the recipe is good, and his private sensual delights need not affect your own more immediate pleasure, some night with a friend or two and a chafing dish, for instance:

Hang Town Fry
(*from the* Sunset Cook Book)

Drain and pat dry 2 dozen medium-sized California Eastern [!] oysters, season them with salt and pepper and roll first in flour, then in beaten egg, and then in fine white bread-crumbs. Put them into a hot frying-pan with melted butter, and fry to a golden brown on one side; before turning them over pour over all 4 or 5 whole eggs beaten light. Let cook a minute, then turn over and brown on other side to color them just as desired. The resulting dish will look like an egg pancake with oysters mixed in. Serve 2 or 3 links of tiny browned breakfast sausages and shoestring potatoes with Hang Town Fry.

Another man, Bob Davis, who writes with coherent enthusiasm of "a few intrepid souls who have time to cook and who approach the task with pride," tells briefly but clearly in Armitage's *Fit for a King* about a bayman's home on the marshes of Massapequa, on Long Island, where one chill fall afternoon he went duck hunting with someone.

"The housewife asked us if we liked onions . . . 'Yes' . . . and if we liked oysters . . . 'Yes' . . . and at once disappeared into the kitchen. In fifteen minutes we had our gum boots under the table and both our elbows on top. Bad manners, but good cooking. I secured the recipe. Here it is":

(And Mr. Davis's recipe seems given in the same voluptuous generous way that makes such men as he say, "That . . . now *that* was the best thing I ever ate in my life . . .")

Oysters and Onions

Slice enough small white onions to cover half an inch in depth the bottom of a skillet; pour half a pint of oyster juice over all and let simmer until onions become transparent. Add pepper and salt and a tablespoonful of butter; cook until butter melts. Spread over onion base a solid blanket of blue point oysters . . . about forty . . . and cook with lid off for five minutes. Place lid on and cook until oysters begin to scallop. Serve on toast with pancake turner, so as not to disarrange the layer. . . . No duck hunter who pretends to be half a man can face the crack of gray dawn better equipped.

That is one man's decision, of course. I know of another, who faced the gray dawn once in a Chesapeake Bay inlet as big as a buttonhole, where he hid from a howling wind when he and another little boy got stormbound in their boat.

They rocked quietly all night, while the air moaned above them, and in the morning they saw that they were floating above oysterbeds as perfect as something in a dream.

They pulled off their clothes and swam down through the stilled water, and brought up oysters bigger than their hands, and sat there in the cool fresh grayness of the dawn, cracking open the shells and sucking down the firm fish within. When each little boy had emptied his shells, he dove down for more, and all the hidden fears of the hard night vanished as they ate, and dove, and ate, naked as they were born in the growing light.

The end of the story was that a bullet plunked into their little cabin wall, because they were stealing oysters from one of the most famous privately owned beds of the most delicious strain of the whole Atlantic Coast. The guard frightened them, and then pitied them and let them go, and they headed into the bay full of the best breakfast they were ever to eat in their lives, wiser but not sadder little boys.

Index of Recipes